The Newborn Baby Manual

Your Guide to Hospital Childbirth, Postpartum
Recovery, and Caring for Your New Baby

Carly Rabazinski, BSN, RNC-MNN

Disclaimer

The information provided in this book is designed to provide helpful information on the subjects discussed. This book is not meant to be used, nor should it be used, to diagnose or treat any medical condition. For diagnosis or treatment of any medical problem, consult your own physician. The publisher and author are not responsible for any specific health or allergy needs that may require medical supervision and are not liable for any damages or negative consequences from any treatment, action, application or preparation, to any person reading or following the information in this book. References are provided for informational purposes only and do not constitute endorsement of any websites or other sources. Readers should be aware that the websites listed in this book may change. This book contains affiliate links. I may make a small commission if you click affiliate links. Thank you for your support!

Table of Contents

Introduction

"Well, they don't send you home from the hospital with a manual!"

If you are pregnant or recently had a baby, chances are pretty good that you've heard some version of this statement from at least one person. People love to remind terrified new parents that, once you leave the hospital, *you're on your own.*

That is why I decided to write this book. I figured, if the hospitals aren't going to start passing out a handbook that teaches new parents how to take care of a newborn baby, somebody better write one! On top of that, I feel that women **want** to be prepared before giving birth, but there are not a ton of resources out there that come from the perspective of a medical professional that knows exactly what you can expect, and what you should know **before** you go into labor.

So, who am I?

I'm glad you asked. I am a registered nurse with a Bachelor of Science in nursing, and I have years of postpartum (also called *mother/baby*) hospital nursing experience under my belt. I am also a certified Maternal Newborn Nurse. To put it simply, newborn babies and their mom's *are my specialty*. I have also recently graduated from the New Parent Club (and am currently navigating the stormy seas of toddler parenting).

I know all too well the overwhelming amount of information that they *do* give you before you leave the hospital. Typically, you're so ready to get out of there that the mound of instructions they give you end up getting stuffed in a diaper bag and you immediately forget everything the discharge nurse said by the time you make it to the parking lot.

By Day 2 at home you're thinking, "Um...what do I do now?!" And that's exactly where this book comes in handy.

I'm going to share the need-to-know information, with some helpful tips I learned not only from my experience as a postpartum nurse, but as a new mom. I'm not just covering newborn care, though. **It is just as important that you are prepared to care for yourself, too!** I am covering the most important information you should know about childbirth in a hospital setting, as well as caring for yourself during the postpartum period. My hope is that you will read this book *before* you go into labor- think of it as your homework while pregnant. That way, you can go into the hospital feeling totally prepared, educated and ready.

Pregnancy is hard, labor is harder, and being a parent is the ultimate challenge- but knowledge is power. Arming yourself with the essential information (and none of the "extra" stuff that you don't have time for) is the best thing you can do before entering this next chapter of your life. You can visit my website, www.nurse-carly.com, where I discuss all things pregnancy, childbirth, postpartum and newborn care.

PART 1:
Childbirth in a Hospital

Having a C-Section

You might be thinking, "Well, I'll just go ahead and skip over this section, I'm not having a C-section!" I'd like to stop you right there and urge you to read this- no matter *what* your birth plan is, and I'll tell you exactly why.

Yes, it is true- there are several circumstances that can arise in which you might be required to have a scheduled C-section. However, most pregnant women go into the hospital assuming they will have a vaginal birth, but things do not always go as planned.

In my nursing experience, I always found that patients that had an emergency or unplanned C-section seemed to have a much harder recovery, in general. I attribute this to a complete lack of education about the surgery itself, as well as being unprepared for the intense recovery- which makes total sense! I want to give you all the nitty gritty details about this major surgery so that if you do end up needing a C-section, you will know exactly what to expect.

Before Surgery

If you are having a scheduled C-section, you will be given a specific time to arrive at the hospital. You will not be permitted to eat or drink for at least 12 hours prior to your surgery time. Once you are checked in, you will change into a hospital gown, and have an IV inserted in your hand or arm. Typically, your epidural will be placed once you are wheeled into the operating room, followed by a Foley catheter inserted into your urethra to drain your urine from your bladder (you won't feel this if they have already started the epidural). You may be "clipped" or shaved down below. If you have an unplanned C-section, these things will all still be done, but much faster.

After the surgery, you will be wheeled into a recovery area for about 2 hours. Depending on how you personally handle anesthesia medications, you may feel nauseous or even throw up- if so, they will give you medication through your IV to try to stop it. You will be allowed to have ice chips at this point. After you recover for about 2 hours, you will be taken to the postpartum floor (if this is available at your hospital) which is where you will stay for about 3 days.

Pain Control After C-section

Pain control will likely differ from hospital to hospital, but the basics are the same. Always ask your doctor ahead of time what their typical plan of action is for pain control, so that you are familiar with your options. I will tell you the *most likely* options for pain control.

You may have an epidural catheter in your back with what I will call "heavy duty" pain medication running on a button system- this gives you a continuous small dose, and then you can press the button yourself for an extra dose every 20 minutes or so, for up to 24 hours. In some cases, they may use a different type of medication, called Duramorph, where the epidural effects last for 24 hours, without the actual epidural catheter in place. If this is the case for you, the epidural catheter would be removed while you are in recovery.

If you are feeling pain even with the epidural, which is called *breakthrough pain*, there is typically the option to give you additional, non-narcotic pain medication. You may be offered Toradol, which is a stronger, IV-form of ibuprofen (which you may know by the brand names Advil or Motrin), given every 6 hours. You may also be offered acetaminophen (brand name: Tylenol) via IV. It is unlikely that you will be given medication by mouth during this time- you must be able to tolerate liquid and food before you can be switched from IV medication to pills, and you won't be allowed to eat solid food for either a certain number of hours, or until the nurse or doctor is able to hear bowel sounds when they listen to your abdomen (more on this later).

After you have eaten some real food, the epidural will be discontinued. Discontinuing the epidural simply means means disconnecting the tubing from the machine- you may still have the catheter in your back until a member of the anesthesia team comes to remove it. Removing the epidural catheter is a quick, painless situation- the worst part is when they have to remove the tape that holds it in place. At this point, you may be offered (depending on your personal history) 1-2 tabs of Percocet (which is oxycodone mixed with acetaminophen) or oxycodone by itself, which you can have every 4 hours, and a high dose ibuprofen every 6-8 hours.

Now, for some advice from your personal nurse: I have had **many** patients that refuse to take pain medication once they are off the epidural. When the epidural is first discontinued, you still have that heavy duty medication in your system, so, naturally, you might feel great. This gives patients a false sense of pain control. What typically happens (and I mean, like clockwork), is a few hours after the epidural is discontinued and the patient has refused additional medication, the pain comes on with a vengeance. The problem with this is that once that pain threshold is reached, it is difficult to get it back down to a tolerable level with oral medication, because it takes a while for that to get through your system. These patients, to put it bluntly, are *miserable*.

I understand that many women are afraid to take the narcotic pain medication, and that's okay, but I do not recommend skipping the ibuprofen and/or acetaminophen. In some cases, these medications alone will not control the pain, so additional relief may be necessary (in the first 48 hours). Many providers are no longer sending their patients home with a prescription for narcotics after a C-section, so it should be your goal to be done with those medications by the time you are discharged from the hospital. It is also worth noting that the typical pain medications given following a C-section are considered safe for breastfeeding because it crosses into the milk in such small doses. However, I would certainly recommend that you verify this with your provider and/or a lactation consultant.

Eating After C-section

Typically, you will be placed on a clear liquid diet once you are on the postpartum or recovery floor, and they will let you slowly advance it from clear liquid (water, chicken broth, etc.), to full liquid (thicker soups), then to a soft regular diet (very little difference from a normal diet), and then finally to a regular diet- all depending on whether or not you have any nausea/vomiting with each advancement. If you do, you will not advance your diet further until things are settled. This process of advancing the diet can take several hours. However, some providers are okay with allowing patients to being eating a normal diet once bowel sounds are present. It is wise to avoid heavy or greasy foods for the first few days following surgery.

Peeing After C-section

You will have a Foley catheter placed in your urethra before surgery- this is usually done after you are already numb, so don't worry about feeling it go in. The catheter will drain any urine from your bladder down a tube and into an attached bag. This will stay in place until you are able to get out of bed, which is recommended at 12 hours post-surgery.

Once the catheter is removed, you need to be able to pee in the toilet- usually within 6 hours. In rare circumstances, you may not be able to pee, which is a temporary side effect. In this case, your nurse may need to use what is called a "straight catheter" to remove the urine from your bladder. Drink plenty of water and do not wait until it feels like you have to pee really bad. You should try to get up every 1-2 hours to pee. This 1-2 hour rule still applies even *after* you meet the goal of peeing the first time after the catheter is removed- you need to continue to get up and pee often, because if your bladder gets too full, it pushes on your uterus, which can cause excess bleeding. An empty bladder equals a happy postpartum uterus.

Bleeding After C-section

A lot of my first-time C-section patients are shocked that they have vaginal bleeding afterwards, so this is always good info to have beforehand! When you first get to the postpartum or recovery floor, they will have you laying on absorbent pads or towels, and the nurse will clean you up every so often. You may feel some "gushes" every now and then, especially once you start breastfeeding or pumping. Breastfeeding/pumping stimulates the uterus to contract, just like in labor, so it can cause a little extra bleeding in the beginning.

Once you are able to walk, you will be given mesh underwear and large pads to wear. There can appear to be a lot of bleeding right after a C-section, mainly because the blood pools internally while you are laying down- the first few times you get up it can look a little scary. The rule of thumb is that your bleeding **should not saturate (meaning 100% soaked) 1 pad within 1 hour.** If it does, call your nurse so she can see for herself. The nurse will also be pressing on your uterus to make sure it's firm: a soft uterus = too much bleeding. The bleeding lightens up each day, and is usually gone in the first few weeks after delivery.

Walking After C-section

As I mentioned, the earlier you are able to get out of bed, the better for your recovery. The nurses and doctors will recommend it around 12 hours after surgery. However, if you feel up to it before the 12-hour mark, then, by all means- get movin'! The first time you get up, it should be with the help of your nurse, to make sure you are stable on your feet, and also to help you push your IV pole (if you still have one). She will either have you walk to the bathroom to get new underwear and pads in place, or she will put the underwear on you while you are in bed. This probably sounds a little invasive, but I promise, the nurses think nothing of it. It's just part of the postpartum experience!

Showering After C-section

There are a few factors at play when it comes to your first shower after surgery. If you still have your epidural, you won't be able to shower until it is completely removed. If your incision has a dressing, you may not be able to shower until it is removed (this depends on the doctor). Some doctors don't use dressings at all, and if that's the case for you, then you just have to wait until your epidural is out.

When you do shower, do not scrub your incision- just let the water run over it. Most importantly, pat dry as much excess water as you can from the incision. You want to keep it completely dry.

Activity and General Recovery After a C-Section

The biggest takeaway from your discharge instructions after having a C-section should be this: take it easy. This is not a suggestion. I know that it is very difficult as a new mom, and sometimes, as a mother of multiple children, to be expected to do such foreign tasks as relaxing and doing nothing, but this really is important for your recovery. It is very common for C-section patients to overexert themselves and create complications, such as an opened incision, excess bleeding or even infection. Listen to your body, rest as much as you possibly can, and don't be afraid to ask your loved ones for help. This is the rule for the first two weeks after surgery, at the very least. It will take up to 6 weeks for your incision to fully heal, and for your body to be returning to a normal state.

Vaginal Birth

For first-time moms, the thought of vaginal birth is probably the most anxiety-provoking, fear-filled part of pregnancy. I know- I've been there. However, just as with a C-section, I feel that knowing at least the basics of what to expect from the experience can help you to feel more at ease with the process, and allow you to focus on the main goal- getting that baby out!

Pain Control During and After Vaginal Delivery

Every pregnant woman's top question: how much is this gonna hurt, and how do I make it *not* hurt? There are a few different options when it comes to pain control during a vaginal delivery.

1. **Epidural**

   This is obviously the most popular method of pain control during a vaginal delivery. In most cases, it is up to you when you want to have the epidural placed. The only time it's not up to you is if you are too far dilated (getting close to 10cm) and they won't have time to put it in. I would like to offer my own personal piece of advice regarding the timing of the epidural: try to wait as long as you can, if your labor is progressing at a normal rate (not too fast). It may not the best plan of action to walk into the hospital at 1cm and immediately get the epidural. Try your best to give your body time to feel the contractions and do the work the hard way, with you being free to walk around, bounce on a birthing ball, sit on the toilet, etc. Once the epidural is in, you are stuck in bed, which really isn't ideal for the labor and dilation process.

2. **Walking Epidural**

This is basically a low dose epidural, meaning that you have enough feeling in your lower half that you can, hypothetically, still walk around. There are some caveats to this option. The first is that although the idea is to avoid numbing the lower half enough so that you can walk, it doesn't always work out that way. You may still be too numb to walk around normally. Second, this type of epidural requires closer monitoring and assistance with any movement, due to the increased potential for falls/injury.

3. **IV Pain Medication**

You may have the option to receive IV narcotics for pain control during labor. However, this does have the potential to cause complications for the baby. Talk to your doctor about your options for IV pain control during labor.

4. **Using a Doula**

If you're looking for a natural alternative for pain control, I would recommend looking into hiring a doula. Research has shown that women that have a doula present are more likely to have a natural birth.

Most women only require mild pain medication after vaginal delivery, such as ibuprofen and/or acetaminophen. These medications will help with the pain and swelling of the perineal area. Another source of pain that you might not be expecting is due to what is called *afterbirth pain*. This is caused by the uterus contracting after delivery in order to start returning to its pre-pregnancy size, and for some women, this pain can be as intense as contractions during labor! Afterbirth pains are typically more intense with each child, so the more babies you have had, the stronger you can expect these postpartum pains to be. The pain from the contracting uterus can also be treated with ibuprofen. For most women, the pains only lasts for the first few days after delivery.

Eating During and After Vaginal Delivery

In most hospital systems, once you are admitted to have your baby, that's the end of eating and drinking until baby arrives. Typically, you can have ice chips, and maybe some sips of fluids every now and then. It's not fun, but it is part of delivering a baby in the hospital.

The medical rationale behind this idea is this: if you were to need an emergency C-section and be placed under anesthesia, there is a risk that a full stomach could cause you to vomit and then *aspirate*, or breathe in, that vomit, which would obviously be a problem. There is a large debate about this rule, so I would recommend speaking to your provider about their thoughts on eating and drinking small amounts throughout labor. The good news is, unlike a C-section, you can eat and drink whatever you want right after you deliver!

Peeing During and After Vaginal Delivery

Your ability to pee while in labor will depend largely on whether or not you have an epidural. If you do not have one, you will be free to walk around the room and use the bathroom. In fact, some women find it helpful to sit on the toilet during contractions. If you do have an epidural, you will be confined to your bed, and therefore, a Foley catheter will most likely be placed to drain your urine from your bladder (you won't even know it's there). After a vaginal delivery, you will be escorted to the bathroom to ensure that you don't have any issues peeing.

In some cases, you might have difficulty, due to the effects of the epidural or possible swelling, so you may need a straight catheter (a small tube that goes into the urethra to drain urine from the bladder and is then removed). However, in most cases, peeing is not an issue. During this first trip to the bathroom, your nurse may assist you with what is called "peri-care" — the act of "cleaning up" down there after birth. You should be given a squirt bottle to fill with warm water, which you will use each time you go to the bathroom to ensure the area is clean, especially if you required stitches. You will also be given some mesh underwear and a very large pad for bleeding.

Bleeding After Vaginal Delivery

There will be a good amount of bleeding and amniotic fluid released immediately following delivery. A few minutes after you deliver, the nurse will press on your uterus to expel any clots and also to help your uterus firm up. A firm, contracted uterus is of the utmost importance in the hours and days following delivery- a "boggy" (I despise this word, but that's what we use), or non-firm uterus, leads to heavy bleeding and subsequent complications, so your uterus will be pressed on quite often during your hospital stay. It is uncomfortable, but brief. Your nurse should be monitoring your bleeding following delivery. The rule of thumb is that you should not saturate (100% soak) 1 pad in 1 hour. If this happens, call your nurse so she can assess your bleeding. I discuss this in more detail in the C-section chapter, and the Postpartum Hemorrhage chapter.

Tearing and Stitches

Did you skip all the other chapters and come straight here?

I think tearing during childbirth has got to be the number one concern among soon-to-be mothers- with pooping during birth coming in at a close second (I'll save you the Google time- I've been told by labor nurses that *not* pooping while pushing is a one-in-a-million occurrence). As much as I hate to tell you this, tearing is pretty darn common, too, especially among first-time mothers.

Any damage that is incurred during the exit of your baby from the birth canal is evaluated by the physician or midwife, and graded on a scale, as follows:

1. **Lacerations:**

    Less severe than tears, lacerations are possible in many areas of the vaginal region, including inside the vagina, on the labia or around the urethra. These are typically able to heal quickly on their own (without stitches) and may only cause slight discomfort or burning during urination.

2. **1st Degree:**

14

A first degree tear is the least severe, and involves the perineal skin (the perineum is the space between the vaginal opening and the rectum) and some tissue underneath it. A few stitches may be needed.

3. **2nd Degree:**

   A second degree tear goes slightly deeper, involving the skin and perineal muscle. Stitches are required.

4. **3rd Degree:**

   A third degree tear extends into the anal sphincter, which is the ring of muscle surrounding the anus. Stitches are required.

5. **4th Degree:**

   A fourth degree tear is the most severe, and we nurses have a term for it: *tore up from the floor up.* In other words, the tear extends into the anal mucosa. This type of tear usually requires a more extensive repair, sometimes in the operating room. If it makes you feel better, I have only seen a handful of these in my nursing career.

6. **Episiotomy:**

   An episiotomy is when the provider uses a scalpel to create a small incision in the perineum. It is sometimes performed during the pushing phase to assist with the release of the baby's head. Episiotomies are being performed less than in the past, but it is a good idea to discuss this procedure with your provider at one of your later OB appointments, and find out their general policy about when they are performed. Episiotomies do require stitches.

Medications for Perineal Injury Pain Control

Depending on the degree of your tear, you may be fine taking ibuprofen and/or acetaminophen for pain and swelling- ask your doctor for the appropriate dosage. However, a more extensive repair may require some heavier medication, such as Percocet (acetaminophen combined with oxycodone), at least for the first day or so, which can be provided by your doctor while you are in the hospital.

Other methods of pain control for perineal injury include:

- **Ice packs:** These are the most useful in the first 24 hours following delivery; after that, they aren't as helpful for reducing swelling and pain.

- **Pericare bottle:** Using your bottle filled with warm water is actually quite comforting to the area and helps to keep it clean after using the restroom.

- **Epifoam:** this is a steroid foam that can be applied a few times a day to reduce pain and swelling. It should be available at the hospital, so ask your nurse, if she doesn't bring it to you first.

- **Dermoplast:** This is an aerosol numbing spray (benzocaine) that helps to alleviate the stinging around the stitches. This should also be available at the hospital, but if not, you can get it at most drug stores or on Amazon.

- **Tuck's:** Tuck's pads are soaked in witch hazel, which is excellent for calming labial swelling, and especially great for relieving hemorrhoids. Did I forget to mention hemorrhoids? If you've never had them before, there's a solid chance you'll have them after a vaginal delivery. These should be given in the hospital, but they are also available at most drug stores.

Activity and General Recovery from Vaginal Delivery

One of the greatest upsides of having a vaginal delivery is the speedy recovery afterwards. Unlike a C-section, you are generally able to be up and moving around somewhat normally just a few hours after giving birth. If you don't have an epidural, it's even faster than that!

During the first few days, up to around 2 weeks after delivery, you will experience some generalized soreness and possible stinging or burning (mainly when you pee). Sitting down will be uncomfortable for the first few days, so be extra careful when plopping down on a couch or chair. It may be helpful to sit on pillows. Continue using the pain control items mentioned previously (Dermoplast, ibuprofen or acetaminophen as prescribed, pericare bottle, and Tuck's pads) until you are feeling better down below.

Full healing takes around 6 weeks, and you must wait until you are cleared by your doctor or midwife to get back to sexual intercourse. Even at that point, sex may be painful, so listen to your body and go slowly.

Postpartum Hemorrhage

There is one very scary reality about childbirth that I must educate you about. Again, not to scare you- to prepare you, so that you can be your own advocate, and also know exactly what to look out for and what you can do about it.

Postpartum hemorrhage is excessive bleeding after delivery, measured as greater than 500mL after vaginal delivery or greater than 1000mL after C-section. It is most likely to occur in the first 24 hours after delivery, but **it is possible to hemorrhage up to twelve weeks postpartum**. Postpartum hemorrhage is the leading cause of maternal death in the United States, and part of the reason behind that statistic is because many times, it gets overlooked. There are many things that can place you at higher risk for having a postpartum hemorrhage, but to name a few: history of hemorrhage with previous delivery, having a C-section, blood disorders, certain ethnicities, infection, obesity, or preeclampsia.

As I mentioned previously, the rule of thumb for your bleeding is that it should not saturate 1 pad within 1 hour. Like I've told you, you should be getting up often in the first few days after birth to go pee (remember, empty bladder = happy uterus), so that is when you should also be taking note of your bleeding. If you are saturating 1 pad in 1 hour, immediately call your nurse. She may assess you- check the bleeding herself, feel your uterus to see if it is firm, check your vital signs (blood pressure, heart rate, respirations)- if she does not do these things, do not be afraid to ask her to do them. If she still doesn't do them, ask to see the charge nurse. And this rule goes for any time you are feeling uncomfortable with your care, or as though your nurse is not taking you seriously.

It is unfortunate, but not all nurses are equal- just as there are **excellent** nurses in the hospital system, there are also bad ones, and it really is the luck of the draw for you, as the patient. You know yourself better than anyone. If something just doesn't feel right, demand action.

Another sign to watch for regarding hemorrhage is clots. It is normal and somewhat common to find a few small clots on your pad, or feel them come out into the toilet when you pee (they'll look like dark lumps, for lack of a better description). If you pass a large clot, the size of a golf ball or larger, or if you have lots of clots coming out, call your nurse. Again, she should assess you and decide whether or not the physician needs to be notified. Sometimes, these clots signify that there may be an internal issue- such as a piece of the placenta being left behind in the uterus, which results in the uterus not being able to contract properly. Your doctor may need to investigate further.

Other symptoms of possible hemorrhage:

- Low blood pressure (less than 90/50) and high heart rate (above 100)

- Low urine output- either your Foley catheter has very little urine in it (should be at least 30mL's per hour) or you are not needing to pee often, which is unusual for a postpartum patient

- Feeling dizzy, lightheaded

Again, I will reiterate: if symptoms are present, or you just don't feel "right", call your nurse. If actions are not taken to assess you and figure out the cause of the problem, demand to see the charge nurse, and if that doesn't solve anything, demand that someone call your physician and let them know that you want to be seen immediately. You are in control of your care. Don't be afraid to speak up.

PART 2:
Newborn Care

Umbilical Cord

The umbilical cord is the part that attaches to the placenta and helps bring essential nutrients to your growing baby for 9 months. I have to include that part because there is a surprising number of new parents that are not exactly sure what the umbilical cord is even doing there in the first place, so, now you know.

The umbilical-cord related knowledge most parents *are* already aware of is the part where the doctor asks someone to cut the cord. The cord will be clamped off with a special plastic, well, *cord clamp-* a very aptly-named tool. While you are in the hospital, the piece of the umbilical cord that remains attached to your baby's stomach will be a little moist and "jelly-like" to the touch, usually for the first day or so, and then it will begin to start drying out. By the time you are ready to leave the hospital, the cord will be a dark, brownish-black, and it may have a plastic-like appearance.

The cord clamp should be removed while you are in the hospital, usually on Day 2, but definitely before you go home. Sometimes, this task does get overlooked, so be sure to double-check that the clamp is removed before you leave. If you don't notice the clamp until you get home, just be sure the pediatrician removes it at your baby's follow-up appointment, which is typically 24-48 hours after you are discharged from the hospital.

Your nurse or the pediatrician in the hospital should teach you about caring for the umbilical cord- the instructions for this *used to* include using rubbing alcohol on a cotton ball or Q-tip to clean around the cord and help it dry out, but this practice is now considered to be "old school". Some doctors and nurses still teach it, but more recent research has shown that this practice doesn't help the cord dry out any faster, and, instead, it may prevent the cord from detaching naturally (Mayo Clinic, 2018). So, skip the rubbing alcohol and stick to simple warm water and a mild soap- something specially formulated for newborn skin. Use this solution once per day to clean **around** the cord, and/or clean up any poop or pee that happens to get on the area during a diaper change. The most important thing is to be sure to keep the cord and the skin around it clean and dry.

Check the cord and the surrounding skin daily to look for these symptoms:

- Excessive redness
- Swelling
- Foul odor
- Discharge or pus
- Bleeding
- The cord has not fallen off by 3 weeks after birth

If any of these symptoms are present, call your pediatrician.

In about 8-10 days after birth, the leftover cord will simply detach and fall off on it's own. When this happens, the belly button may have a little discharge or "wetness" to it at first, so continue cleaning with soap and water daily and keeping it dry until the area is completely healed. **Do not** attempt to remove the cord stump yourself.

Diapers

Diapers are probably one of the most intimidating parts of new parenthood, but the funny thing is, you'll be an absolute pro in about 2 days flat — I promise.

Tips for Diaper Changes

- Babies are fragile, but not so fragile that you can't move them at all during a diaper change. They kick and wiggle a lot, which can pose an extra challenge, so you will have to gently hold their legs while wiping and putting the new diaper underneath them.

- For baby girls, always wipe front to back (or starting at the top and wiping towards their butt). Women [should] know this already, but this is new information for the dads out there. Going the opposite way will push bad bacteria towards their urethra (where they pee) and can cause bladder infections.

- For baby boys, be sure to clean the tip of the penis, especially after circumcision.

- When the diaper is off and they feel the cold air after being wet, it triggers them to pee (more typical for boys but girls do it, too), so be on high alert when you first take the diaper off- it helps to use another diaper to cover them up so you don't get peed on.

Paying attention to the number of pee and poop diapers your baby has each day is absolutely critical, especially in the first month. This is how you ensure that they are eating enough. My favorite brand of diapers is Pampers Swaddlers, not only because they've never failed me in the leak department, but because they have a built-in line down the front of the diaper that turns blue when it's wet- very helpful for knowing exactly what's going on without having to peek inside.

In the first few days of life, you may notice an orange-colored stain in your baby's diaper, especially if you are breastfeeding- this is sometimes referred to as "brick dust", and is usually a normal finding. The discoloration is urate crystals, which is the end product of uric acid- a normal product of metabolism. Babies are born with a high concentration of uric acid in their bloodstream, and if they are breastfeeding exclusively in the first few days, these crystals are more concentrated and noticeable in the diaper. If it persists passed the first few days or your baby is not having enough wet diapers per day, this can be a sign of dehydration, and you should call the pediatrician immediately.

Speaking of wet diapers, a good rule of thumb for counting how many your baby is having per day is to correlate it with how many days old your baby is. In the first 12-24 hours after birth, it is only expected for your baby to pee **at least once**. By Day 3, your baby should have at least 3 wet diapers in 24 hours, by Day 6, at least six wet diapers, etc. It tends to cap off at around at least 6 wet diapers in 24 hours after the first week of life. It is important to remember that wet diapers are the most important measure for indicating the eating and hydration status of your baby. **If your baby has not had a wet diaper in 24 hours, you must call the pediatrician.**

Poop diapers have slightly different rules, but should still be monitored closely. In the first 24 hours, your baby will likely have their first poop, which is called *meconium.* It will be a black, sticky substance with no odor. The poop will gradually transition from black to a yellowish color over the first few days of life. Newborn poop can go through a variety of colors, so don't be alarmed if you open the diaper to find bright green poop. No, they probably did not eat a box of green crayons when you weren't looking. Poop color and consistency will also vary depending on whether baby is breastfeeding or formula feeding. Breastfed babies tend to have more loose and frequent stools, while formula fed babies will have slightly more formed, "pasty" poop that is less frequent (are we having fun yet?)

While many newborns poop several times per day, it is not uncommon to expect only 1 dirty diaper in 24 hours. It is also not uncommon for a baby to go a full 24 hours without a poop diaper. Always assess your baby's "signs"- if they appear especially fussy or have a rigid tummy, they may be constipated, which warrants a call to the pediatrician.

Bathing

Newborn bathing is another experience that can be a little intimidating at first, but, as with all things in parenthood, you'll get the hang of it.

The first bath is typically done in the hospital by a nurse. Each hospital is different, but, as long as there are no special circumstances surrounding the birth or the baby's health, there should be no reason that you, as the parent or parents, can't attend the first bath, or even assist the nurse. All you have to do is ask. I highly encourage you to do so, because you will want to watch how the nurse bathes the baby so you can do it yourself at home.

Some hospitals are now practicing "delayed bathing", which is waiting a certain number of hours (between 7-24 hours) after delivery to give the first bath. The rationale for this is to allow the newborn time to stay skin-to-skin with mom or dad (which helps to regulate temperature, heart rate, breathing and even blood sugar levels), and also to avoid messing with their temperature and blood sugar by exposing them to cold. Current research also shows that delaying the first bath increases rates of breastfeeding. Some parents are really not on board with this idea, but I do recommend delaying the first bath for at least 12 hours after birth.

Contrary to popular belief, babies don't really get "dirty", unless it's from obvious causes, like spit-up, an explosive diaper, or a toddler sibling that decided to color their new baby with green marker. They do not require daily bathing- in fact, in can be harmful to bathe newborns so often, due to their delicate skin that dries out easily. Plan on bathing your baby once every 2-3 days, unless one of the previously mentioned scenarios takes place. You should have a newborn bathtub that fits in your sink or in your own bathtub. Always test the water temperature first- it should not feel hot to you. Use a mild soap specially formulated for newborns, and be sure to rinse all the soap off. Be sure to keep all crevices dry after the bath. I remember being horrified when I realized my baby's armpit had developed some sort of seeping rash, simply because I forgot to dry under there! I always recommend following bath time with a gentle baby lotion to keep their skin hydrated.

Sleeping

Ah, yes. Sleep. Every new parent's most-Googled topic, I'm sure.

The first thing you should know is that newborn babies are made to sleep. It's really all they're supposed to be doing- about 18 hours a day! The catch is, they still have to eat, because that's the other part of their job. If you haven't figured it out by now, newborns eat quite often. Therefore, your newborn will most likely be sleeping for short stretches, waking every 2-3 hours to eat. We will cover feedings in another chapter, but your baby should be eating 8-12 times in 24 hours.

The most common thing new parents are concerned about is their baby sleeping at night, because, *duh*. There are many factors that can contribute to your baby's sleeping pattern, and every baby is different- but a large factor that will determine your baby sleeping at night is whether they are formula-fed or breastfed. Breast milk digests faster, therefore, exclusively breastfed newborns will eat more often than formula-fed newborns. Formula digests slower, which results in longer stretches between meals- typically 3-4 hours. This information is not meant to discourage you from breastfeeding, it's just the way it works!

Now, I've already mentioned that the goal is to reach 8-12 feedings in 24 hours. Have you ever heard the saying, "Never wake a sleeping baby"? Well, that is definitely true when it applies to nighttime! If your baby is sleeping for longer stretches at night and not waking up to eat, leave them alone and count your lucky stars. You will just need to be sure they are making up for the lost feeds during the daytime, which is completely doable.

When it comes to all the hype around "sleep training" and teaching your baby how to sleep, my best advice is to ignore it when you have a newborn. Newborn babies are not meant to sleep through the entire night- all newborn babies eat *at least* once during the night. This is just temporary, and it is something all parents have to deal with. When your baby is around 4-6 months old, that is when you can start entertaining the idea of dropping the night time feeding.

The Bedtime Routine

The greatest advice I could possibly give to new parents is to establish a bedtime routine. This was the single best thing my husband and I did with our newborn, and it has paid off greatly. From the time we brought her home, we did the same things every night starting at 5PM:

- bath (if it was a bath night)

- lotion + jammies

- bottle

- diaper change

- swaddle

- bed at 6PM (she slept in our room in a bassinet for the first several months)

My daughter is almost 3-years-old now, and we have never (knock on wood) had any issues with her sleep, something that I do attribute to her solid routine. Babies (and children, in general) *crave* routine. I can't tell you how many new parents I've talked to or seen out with their baby at 9 or 10 at night, and they'll say things like, "She's just not tired" or "She goes to bed really late". Stop this nonsense! YOU, the parent, are in control of when your baby goes to bed. Bedtime is when *you* say it is. Your baby will adjust to the routine you set.

Other tips for helping your newborn get to sleep at night:

- Quiet environment (if your TV is on, or you and your partner are in the room chatting, that's not gonna work)

- Absolute darkness (babies do not need a night light)

- White noise machine (this simulates the sounds of being in the womb)

- Swaddle (sometimes the involuntary movements of their arms and legs wake them up- swaddling helps them to feel secure)

If your baby is simply not sleeping during the day and/or at night, or is excessively crying and unable to be soothed, you should talk to your pediatrician.

Crying

It probably won't surprise you to hear that crying and newborn babies go hand-in-hand. Many parents become easily frustrated with a crying baby, simply because it is difficult to see your baby in distress, and even more difficult when you can't communicate with them to discover the problem.

It is important to change your viewpoint of your baby's crying. It doesn't mean you're doing a bad job or you have failed because your baby is crying. Their cries *are* their communication, and there are different cries for different needs. The good news is, there is only a handful of possible solutions for your baby's cries, and it isn't too hard to try them all until you pick the right one!

Newborn babies cry for the following reason:

- Hungry
- Wet or dirty diaper
- Tired (Yes, they cry when they need to sleep! It makes no sense!)
- Cold or hot
- Gassy or constipated

I hate that I have to mention this, but it is something we are required to tell parents in the hospital: **never, ever shake a baby, for any reason- including excessive crying.** If you feel the urge to do so, you need to put the baby down and walk away. Shaking a baby even slightly can cause what is called *Shaken Baby Syndrome*, marked by brain damage, seizures, blindness, and/or death.

When to Call The Doctor

As a new parent, it is tempting to call your pediatrician for everything, but this isn't necessary. There are some core signs and symptoms in your newborn that require that call to be made.

- **Not enough wet diapers.** Remember, they should be having about as many wet diapers in 24 hours as days old, tapping out at around 6 per day at 6 days old. Skipping a day or two without a dirty diaper is not nearly as pressing as having no wet diapers in 24 hours. I suggest keeping a diaper log for the first month.

- **Fever.** A fever in a newborn is defined as a temperature of 100.7 or higher. A fever in a newborn is a concern because they have an underdeveloped immune system, so even the smallest infection can pose a bigger problem for them.

- **Poor feeding.** Sometimes your baby will refuse a feeding, and that's normal. If they are refusing multiple feedings in a row- meaning, they just aren't eating- this is a problem.

- **Lethargy.** Babies sleep a lot, we've covered this. There is a difference between sleeping a lot and being lethargic. If your baby is difficult to wake up or seems floppy/weak, call the doctor or 911 immediately.

Coughing, rapid breathing, nasal flaring, or blue lips. The biggest sign your baby can give you that there is something very wrong will begin in their respiratory system. If your baby has a strange sounding cough or wheeze, is breathing faster than 60 breaths per minute (start a timer and count the rises with your hand gently on their belly), the area around their ribcage or chest is "sucking in" when they breathe, their nostrils are flaring in and out, or the area around their mouth and lips is blue, call 911 immediately, as these are signs of possible respiratory distress.

PART 3:
Breastfeeding, Formula Feeding, & Pumping

Introduction to Feeding Your Baby

Newborn feeding is probably the most difficult part about having a newborn- at least, in the beginning. Before you know it, you will have a system in place and a routine figured out, but getting to that point can be a challenge for many new parents. I'm going to give you the need-to-know information to help make feeding your new baby as easy and stress-free as possible.

A note about feeding your baby:

Listen. I have the internet. I know what the dialogue is surrounding the way we choose to feed our babies. I have an enormous amount of knowledge about the benefits of breastfeeding, and have spent countless hours helping new mothers just like you to learn how to feed their baby. You've probably heard the saying "breast is best" at least once in your pregnancy, and I am not at all discounting that. However, in the hospital, we mother/baby nurses have a saying that we share with our patients: *Fed* is best. Yes, there are numerous benefits to breastfeeding your baby, but sometimes it just doesn't work out, for a variety of reasons. And that's OKAY. The most important thing is that you are feeding your baby the nutrition and calories that are vital for their brain development and survival- whether it's at the breast, pumped milk or formula. Do not waste any of your precious time fretting over whether you are able to successfully breastfeed or not. If that baby is fed and happy, you are doing a great job!

The overall goal with all newborn feeding is quite simple:

- Baby is gaining weight at a steady pace (babies typically lose some weight during the first week, and then start gaining back. They should be back to birth weight around Day 10).

- Baby is peeing and pooping regularly (see previous chapter, *Diapers*).

Breastfeeding

You may have been told a time or two that breastfeeding offers both mother and baby a variety of benefits, and this is very true. What you may *not* have been told is that breastfeeding can come with many obstacles, especially in the beginning. I don't tell you this to discourage you from breastfeeding- I simply want you to have the right mindset beforehand. So many of my patients that are first-time mothers are totally *floored* by the difficulty they have initiating and maintaining breastfeeding, and this can lead to unnecessary frustration, self-blame, and fear that they cannot provide for their baby. I want to help you avoid these feelings altogether by being well educated and informed about breastfeeding before you even start. There's a lot to cover here, so let's get to it.

One of the most common misconceptions about breastfeeding and breast milk is that once the baby is born, you immediately have a full supply of breast milk and baby can start chugging away. In reality, after baby is born, your breasts produce very small amounts of a milk-like fluid called *colostrum*. Postpartum nurses and pediatricians call this magical stuff "liquid gold", and for good reason. Although produced in small amounts at a time, colostrum is jam-packed with antibodies and essential nutrients for newborns. Under normal circumstances, your body produces just the right amount of colostrum to nourish your baby for the first several days of life, until your full milk "comes in", usually between days 3-5 (sometimes up to day 7), after birth.

Immediately after your baby is born, they will typically initiate a "first feed" within the first 1-2 hours. This first feeding is usually quite successful, meaning the baby is alert, hungry, searching for the nipple, and latches on without problem. Mothers usually feel very confident after the first feeding, which is wonderful- but let me tell you what happens next. Not much! In the hours following delivery and the first feeding, newborns tend to drift into a very drowsy state. They will spend a lot of the first 24 hours asleep (hopefully skin-to-skin with Mom or Dad!) and may be difficult to feed. Don't panic. As long as there are no signs of *hypoglycemia* (or low blood sugar, something that can sometimes be an issue after birth for a variety of reasons), newborns actually do not require very much nourishment in the first 24 hours. They still have a good supply from being connected to Mom, and may only need a few feedings in the first 24 hours after birth. You should still attempt to feed your baby every 2-3 hours. As far as the length of each feeding, follow your baby's cues. They will let you know they are done by coming off the breast, falling asleep and/or relaxing their hands.

If your baby is having trouble latching onto your breast during this time, again, don't panic. This is very common. Remember, just as you are learning a completely new skill, your baby is also learning- and, just like you, they have also been through a pretty rough day. Keep practicing the latch at each feeding. If you are unable to get baby to latch on, there is a temporary way to feed your baby, using a method called *hand expression.* I highly recommend you do a Google search and find a video demonstrating this technique, but I will provide a guide (from an excellent resource- www.bornandfed.com) below. Hand expressing colostrum and finger-feeding it to your baby is a perfectly acceptable substitute for breastfeeding in the first few days before your full milk comes in, and I highly recommend trying it out.

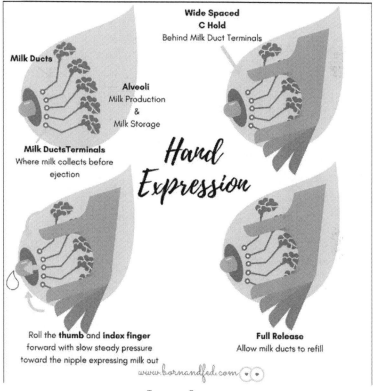

Image Source

Even if your baby is latching on like a champ, I still encourage you to use hand expression when they are not feeding, and I'll tell you why: **your milk supply is built in these crucial first few days after birth**. The more colostrum that is taken out of your breast, the more signals that are sent to your brain to create more milk. If your baby isn't latching, has a weak suck, or your baby is in the NICU and unable to breastfeed, the milk is not being removed, therefore, the brain is being told "no need to send more, there's plenty still here". The brain and the breast work together to figure out exactly how much milk needs to be made for *your* baby, based on how much is being removed. So, the point is, get that milk out however you can, every 2-3 hours- whether it's by the baby eating, hand expressing, or using an electric breast pump.

If you are having any difficulty with breastfeeding- whether it is the latch, getting baby interested feeding, understanding whether they are getting enough, or you just need some reassurance that you are doing it correctly- I urge you to ask for the lactation consultant while you are in the hospital, or contact your local hospital after you leave and ask for information about meeting with a lactation consultant. You might even be able to find one in your area that does home visits. These women are breastfeeding **saints**, and they will make sure your feedings are effective. You can also visit the La Leche League's website for other resources, such as Facebook support groups for breastfeeding: www.llli.org

Complications of Breastfeeding

There are a few things that can go awry with breastfeeding, so it's good to know about them ahead of time.

First, nipple soreness is quite common. You can avoid this two ways:

1. Always ensure that your baby is latched on properly. If baby is sucking only on the end of the nipple, you will become sore very quickly, plus, the feeding will be ineffective. If you have blisters or feel excessively sore, you should contact a lactation consultant or pediatrician for the baby's latch to be evaluated.

2. Use some of your own breast milk to rub on your nipples after each feeding and allow it to air dry. Trust me, it works.

Another complication from breastfeeding is the possibility of an infection of a milk gland, also known as *mastitis*. Mastitis occurs when the gland is not being completely emptied. The leftover milk stays trapped in the gland and infection develops. If you notice that your breast feels hot, tender, red and swollen in one area or you are feeling feverish, you should contact your doctor for evaluation, as you may require antibiotics. Avoid wearing underwire bras while breastfeeding, as this can be a risk factor for mastitis.

Notes about handling breast milk:

- Do not microwave breast milk, as it destroys the composition of the milk. Use a bottle warmer to reheat refrigerated or frozen breast milk.

- Freshly pumped breast milk can be left out at room temperature for up to 6 hours, and refrigerated breast milk can stay out at for up to 4 hours.

- Freshly pumped breast milk can be refrigerated for up to 3 days. It can be frozen for up to 6 months.

- Remember to always date stored milk.

Formula Feeding

There are many reasons a baby might be formula-fed. You may be required to provide formula in the hospital, in the event that your baby's blood sugar level is too low- this is a somewhat common occurrence under certain circumstances, and the baby will be monitored by the doctors and nurses for signs and symptoms. You may choose to give formula because you don't have an interest in breastfeeding, or you might just be supplementing with formula after breastfeeding, under the guidance of a pediatrician and/or lactation consultant. Whatever the reason, there are differences between breast milk and formula, and a few things you should know.

Types of Formula

There are many types of formula available today. In some cases, the pediatrician may recommend a particular type of formula. For example, if your baby showed symptoms of lactose intolerance, the doctor may recommend a soy-based formula. Most of the time, however, the brand you decide to go with is simply a personal choice. I have worked in two different hospital systems that each had a partnership with a certain brand of formula, so do keep in mind that your hospital may only provide one or two brands during your stay. Switching brands is typically not a problem, but you should always consult with your pediatrician first.

The most important thing to know about formula feeding is that formula digests slower than breast milk, so babies will go longer between feedings, usually 3-4 hours (as opposed to 2-3 hours with breast milk). Bottle feeding is much less work for babies compared to breastfeeding, and this is important to know because the first time you give a newborn a bottle, they may guzzle down the entire thing in record time. Parents automatically think, "Oh, wow! They sure were hungry!" which is true, but you want to help pace your baby's bottle feeding.

Newborn Stomach Size

Your breast milk is all your baby needs!

Day One
size of a cherry
5 to 7 ml
1 to 1.5 tsp

Day Three
size of a walnut
22 to 27 ml
.75 to 1 oz

One Week
size of an apricot
45 to 60 ml
1.5 to 2 oz

Two Weeks
size of a large egg
80 to 150 ml
2.5 to 5 oz

Source

49

A newborn's stomach is the size of a cherry and holds only 5-7mL at a time. For reference, the ready-made formula bottles that are typically given to formula-feeding babies in the hospital hold 30mL, or 1 ounce. This is why the nurses and doctors will recommend a maximum of about 10mL's of formula per feeding during the first 24 hours, slowly increasing the amount each day. Going overboard with bottle feedings in the first few days will result in a lot of clean up for you, because it's most likely coming back up.

With that being said, if your baby still seems hungry after these small feedings, you can slowly increase the amount, by about 5mL's, for the next feeding and see how that goes. Newborn feeding is very much trial and error, and you will soon begin to understand your baby's cues that will tell you what they need.

Things to know about formula:

- Use the purest form of water available to mix the formula (tap water is not recommended)

- Read the instructions carefully for mixing formula- you must ensure that you have the correct ratio of water to formula powder for each feeding.

- If you are making batches of formula and storing in the fridge, use a bottle warmer to reheat for each feeding- microwaves can create "hot spots" in the formula which can easily burn baby's mouth.

- Once formula is prepared and the baby has eaten from the bottle, it can only stay out at room temperature for 1 hour before it needs to be thrown away. Bacteria from baby's mouth enters the bottle and can begin growing after the 1-hour mark.

Pumping

You might decide to use a breast pump for a number of reasons: you are planning to go back to work or be separated from your baby, and someone else will need to feed them, you want to have the option of bottle-feeding your breastmilk during the day or night, or maybe you have an oversupply or undersupply of milk. Whatever the reason, pumping adds a different element to feeding your baby, so I want to prepare you.

If you are exclusively pumping, meaning pumped breast milk is the only thing your baby is eating, you will want to pump on the same schedule that your baby would breastfeed, which is typically every 2-3 hours in the beginning. Pumping sessions last about 15 minutes total. If you are exclusively pumping, I highly recommend getting a double electric pump. My personal favorite is the Medela Pump-in-Style Advanced Breastpump. Be sure to check out the chapter *Must-Have Items for You and Your Newborn* to see my other recommendations for pumping essentials.

Supplementing

In certain situations, you might be told by the pediatrician that you need to supplement breastfeeding with bottle feeding either pumped milk or formula. This could be due to a low milk supply, or baby is not on track with weight gain. Basically, baby just needs a little extra, and it's very normal and quite common. The most important thing to remember about supplementing is to always offer the breast milk **first**. If you are breastfeeding, feed your baby at the breast for as long as they want. Once they are finished, supplement with the amount of formula recommended by your pediatrician. If you are pumping, feed the pumped milk first, and separately from the formula. Never mix breast milk with formula.

PART 4:
Postpartum

Sex After Baby

This is another popular topic among new moms, and I am happy to share with you what I know. It is pretty much the standard recommendation that you cannot have intercourse for *at least* 6 weeks following delivery — regardless of whether it was vaginal or a C-section — or until you are cleared by your doctor or midwife during your postpartum visit. You may be overjoyed by this news, or you may be thinking this is just another punishment a la Eve that we females have to bear. Either way, I do not recommend testing the waters before the 6-week mark. Your body needs time to heal, period.

As you may have gathered, having a C-section does have the obvious benefit of sparing your vagina from trauma. But, it does come with the price tag of a more painful recovery period. You may be wondering why you would have to abstain from sex if your vagina wasn't involved, and the reason is because you just had **major abdominal surgery.** Don't push it!

Having a vaginal delivery definitely changes things down below, whether you tear or not. The more involved the repair, the longer it may take for things to heal and feel normal *to you* again. As for men, they're typically happy just to be back in action. Don't stress too much about what they are feeling, as the changes are typically more apparent to you than to them. However, I am happy to report that time heals all wounds, and you should notice improvement after the first 6 months postpartum. If you aren't noticing any improvements, there are things you can do to help the process. See the chapter entitled **Pelvic Floor**.

Unfortunately, things can sometimes go awry in repairs. Not all doctors and midwives are of the same skill level, so first, be sure that you are seeing someone you fully trust with your care, and that has a good track record. If you notice that things don't feel right down there or you are having pain with intercourse after the 6-week mark, be sure to follow-up with your doctor or midwife. In some cases, a revision to the repair may be necessary.

The biggest thing to remember when it comes to postpartum sex is that this is simply a phase in your life. There may be temporary changes in your sex life, but the most important thing is that you must be able to communicate openly with your partner. This is not something that can be ignored or swept under the rug- if you're feeling insecure or not ready, you need to convey those feelings to your partner and keep them in the loop. Shutting out your partner in any way after adding a new baby to the mix is a recipe for disaster. Also, don't be afraid to get help from a licensed therapist if you need guidance on dealing with these changes with your partner. Everyone goes through challenging times in the postpartum period, and you shouldn't feel ashamed. Get help when you need it.

Pelvic Floor

As we have previously discussed, there is physical trauma inflicted during childbirth- whether you have a vaginal delivery or a C-section. What most people don't know is that there can be physical changes to the pelvic floor, regardless of what type of delivery you had. Yes, even C-section mama's can suffer from pelvic floor damage!

The weight of the baby hanging out on these important muscles for 9 months can cause some problems. You may notice in the first few weeks or months after delivery that you have trouble holding your urine. You might leak during physical activity, especially involving running or jumping. Hey, you may even fully pee your pants in public (I'm speaking from experience, people). These are all signs that there has been a change to the pelvic floor.

It is interesting to note that in other countries, postpartum patients are provided with routine pelvic floor rehabilitation. Unfortunately, this is not at all common practice in the United States, so women may have to take this matter into their own hands. Strengthening the pelvic floor is possible in your own home. Personally, I found the Abs, Core and Pelvic Floor program by Natalie Hodson to work wonders, and it is very simple to do over a few weeks. You can also search for pelvic floor exercises on YouTube.

If at-home exercises aren't doing the trick or you think you may have more severe damage, here is a list of resources to help you find a pelvic floor rehabilitation specialist near you:

- American Physical Therapy Association

- International Pelvic Pain Society

- Pelvic Rehab

Boobs After Baby

First thing's first: whether you are or you aren't breastfeeding doesn't really matter to your girls- that milk is comin' in hot whether you plan to use it or not. This usually happens between postpartum Days 3-5, and sometimes as long as up to Day 7. When your milk does come in, you will know it. Your boobs will suddenly feel full, tight, large- basically all the things we've always wanted them to be, am I right?! Except in this version of our dreams, they hurt and also leak milk everywhere. *Ah*, so close.

If you are breastfeeding, your goal should be to keep your boobs emptied on a regular schedule. Letting the milk fill up too much is called *engorgement*, and it can be quite uncomfortable. If you find that you are getting engorged even when keeping baby on a regular feeding schedule, you can choose to pump to relieve the pressure, or even take a hot shower and let the water run over your boobs. This is also great for nipple soreness. Never wear an underwire bra when your breasts are producing milk, as this can lead to a blocked duct. Instead, choose a supportive, seamless style. Using ice packs across your chest for up to 20 minutes every few hours can help relieve the swelling, and over-the-counter ibuprofen may be helpful to alleviate the discomfort.

If you aren't breastfeeding, engorgement will happen in the first few days when your milk comes in. In order to stop the milk from coming in and making you engorged, you have to be sure to stop the release of milk. You can do this by **avoiding** letting the hot water in your shower touch your breasts or nipples (this stimulates a release) and wearing a tight-fitting bra. You can also follow the same tips for discomfort as above- ice packs and over-the-counter ibuprofen to reduce pain and swelling. The milk should gradually stop filling up after a week or so after following these practices.

Nutrition

I t may surprise you to hear that what you eat is highly important, not only while you are pregnant, but in the weeks and months following delivery. If you have a C-section, you will obviously have an incision, which means that your body will be working in overdrive to heal the wound properly. If you have a vaginal delivery, the story is pretty much the same. Although you may not have a large incision like with a C-section, it is likely that you had some type of damage to your tissue, which also sends your body into the heal-this-ASAP mode.

Wound healing requires extra protein, so that should be the focus of your diet in the immediate recovery period. Great sources of protein include chicken, lean red meat, turkey, pork, fish, nuts, seeds, and legumes. Serving sizes of protein should be the size of your fist. You can also try a clean protein powder to ensure you are reaching your protein goal- I highly recommend Orgain Protein Powder in Chocolate Fudge flavor, or Collagen Protein Powder by Primal Kitchen Foods. In addition to a higher protein intake, you will want to be sure to include nutrient-dense, whole foods with each meal.

Examples of whole foods include:

- Leafy greens like spinach, kale, or Swiss chard

- Sweet potatoes

- Beets

- Broccoli

- Cauliflower

- Brussel Sprouts

- Asparagus

Fruit has important nutrients, too, but I recommend limiting your intake to 1 serving per day, and keep the portion size small, about ¼ cup. This is because fruit is high in fructose, which creates a spike in blood sugar.

Fruits to try:

- Strawberries

- Blueberries

- Pineapple

- Mango

- Cantaloupe

- Raspberries

Another must-have in your postpartum diet may surprise you: FAT. Yes, I said it. You need to consume fat to help your body function. We have been taught for years that fat is the enemy, and that is simply untrue. You should add 1-2 tablespoons of healthy fat to each meal. You will probably find that this helps to keep you fuller longer, which is an excellent benefit and will aid in shedding the baby weight!

Examples of healthy fats:

- MCT oil

- Avocado oil

- Olive oil

- Avocado

- Nuts

  Nut butters (almond, cashew, peanut- just be sure the only ingredient is nuts)

  Carbohydrates are also essential for proper bodily functions, cell turnover, and keeping energy levels adequate- however, not all carbs are created equal. Anything made with refined sugar or flour is not going to be helpful. You should still be aware of portion sizes when it comes to healthy carbohydrate foods, because too much of a good thing is real.

Here are some examples of good carbohydrate choices for sustained energy:

- Sweet potatoes

- White potatoes

- Turnips

- Squash- butternut, acorn, yellow, pumpkin

- Zucchini

A rule of thumb that I personally follow, and that helped me lose 65lbs of baby weight, is this: at every meal, your plate (or cup!) should be protein, fiber, healthy fat, and greens. I use this formula (created by the amazing Kelly LeVeque, author of _Body Love_) to make every meal, and I was able to not only lose weight, but feel awesome, which is why I try to share this knowledge with anyone who will listen! If you want to learn more, I highly recommend picking up Kelly's book.

Note: Be sure to sign up for my email list so you will be among the first to know when I release my Postpartum Weight Loss Guide- coming soon!

Postpartum Preeclampsia

You may already be familiar with the term "preeclampsia" from pregnancy or your delivery, as this is a fairly common condition that can develop at any time in pregnancy. Preeclampsia is very high blood pressure in pregnancy that causes certain symptoms, and can lead to *eclamptic seizures*, stroke, organ damage, or death. Unfortunately, the cause of this dangerous condition has not yet been determined.

What most people don't know about preeclampsia is that it is **not** just a condition of pregnancy- **it can occur postpartum.** This makes it even *more* dangerous, because you are more likely to overlook the symptoms during this time. Furthermore, it can take as long as 6 weeks postpartum for the symptoms to appear. If you have any of these symptoms, it is an emergency- call your healthcare provider, and if you can't reach them, call 911 or go to the emergency room immediately. Be sure to tell any emergency staff that you were recently pregnant.

Symptoms of postpartum preeclampsia:

- Severe headache
- Blurred or spotty vision

- Severe abdominal pain

- Nausea/Vomiting

- Swelling of the hands and/or face

- Feeling short of breath

Postpartum Depression

I am thankful that this condition has been gaining much more attention in recent years via social media and television, as this was previously a very silent condition that women dealt with (or didn't deal with) on their own. Postpartum depression affects 25% of women in the first year following childbirth. Please don't get into the mindset of "it won't happen to me", because depression affects **many women**.

So, what is it, exactly? Postpartum depression is a mood disorder that causes extreme feelings of sadness, anxiety, and exhaustion that is different from the typical "I just had a baby" exhaustion. Basically, you just don't feel like yourself, and it's affecting your daily life and your ability to care for yourself and your new baby.

Postpartum depression is different from "baby blues", a term used to describe feelings of sadness in the immediate postpartum period- usually 1-2 weeks after birth. The main difference between the two is that "baby blues" goes away, postpartum depression is more extreme and lingers for longer than 2 weeks after birth. The best thing you can do is to be aware of the symptoms, talk to your partner or support person, and immediately get help.

Symptoms of postpartum depression:

- Extreme feelings of sadness, anxiety, tiredness

- Sleep disturbance (aside from the baby)- either sleeping all the time or not sleeping at all

- Extreme anger

- Avoiding the people you love

- Doubting your ability to care for your new baby

- Thoughts of harming yourself or your baby

There is helpful, efficient treatment available for postpartum depression- you do **not** have to go through this alone. First, call your doctor and report your symptoms. Next, if not already referred by your doctor, reach out to a licensed mental health professional- a therapist, counselor, or psychiatrist- and make an appointment to go and talk to them. You may also be prescribed an antidepressant.

Postpartum depression is due in large part to hormonal imbalances created by the withdrawal of pregnancy hormones, which is how an antidepressant can be helpful- it puts the balance back in place. However, it does take a few weeks to start working, so I recommend seeing a mental health professional in the meantime.

If you or your loved one is thinking about suicide, call 911 and/or The National Suicide Prevention Lifeline: 1-800-273-8255.

When to Call The Doctor

When a new baby has arrived, the parents are typically so concerned with knowing "when to call the doctor" for their little one, that all concern with knowing when to call *your own* doctor goes out the window. I think that our society has such a flippant attitude about childbirth that we tend to consider it as just another day, as if our bodies haven't gone through hell and back and need to be cared for, with close monitoring for signs and symptoms that something might be wrong. I'm going to give you those signs and symptoms right here, so you can reference it if something is worrying you. Don't be afraid to call your doctor or midwife with questions, or ask to be seen if you feel that something is not right.

When to Call the Doctor After a C-Section:

- Temperature of 101 degrees or higher

- Flu-like symptoms: fever, chills, body aches, vomiting, or diarrhea

- Redness, pain, swelling, fresh bleeding or drainage from the incision site

- Sharp abdominal pain

- Increased vaginal bleeding- saturating 1 pad in 1 hour, continuing to pass clots or 1 large clot at a time

- Unexplained nausea/vomiting

- Red, painful, swollen area on the breast

When to Call the Doctor After a Vaginal Delivery:

- Temperature of 101 degrees or higher

- Flu-like symptoms: fever, chills, body aches, vomiting or diarrhea

- Redness, severe pain, swelling, drainage or fresh bleeding from perineal stitches

- Sharp abdominal pain

- Increased vaginal bleeding- saturating 1 pad in 1 hour, continuing to pass clots or 1 large clot at a time

- Unexplained nausea/vomiting

- Red, painful, swollen area on the breast

PART 5:
What You Really Need

I f there is one thing I learned from my pregnancy and life with a newborn, it's that there are a lot of things you absolutely must have- but there is even *more* stuff that you absolutely **do not need**. Nowadays, when I go to a baby shower, I see so many gifts being opened and think to myself, "Nope. Not gonna use that. Ohhh, yeah, that's staying in the box!"

Let me help you avoid filling up your home and precious space with things you really don't need. I have a tried-and-true list of must-haves for a newborn baby that I have shared with my patients *and* anyone I know that is pregnant, and now, I'm going to share it with you!

Must-Have Items for You and Your Newborn

1. Keekaroo Peanut Changer - This is definitely my #1 product. I can't even comprehend doing a diaper change without one of these. You simply wipe it clean when the inevitable extra pee/poo happens, instead of having to remove a cover (like you would use with a traditional foam changing pad) and do laundry all the time.

2. Summer Portable Infant White Noise Machine - You will soon learn that white noise is a **must**. The "shhh" sound reminds the baby of being in the womb, and we found it was so helpful for getting our daughter to sleep. We used this portable machine to attach to the stroller, carseat, and swing during nap times.

3. Dohm Sound Machine - See above. White noise = must-have. This machine is the Mac Daddy of "shhh" machines.

4. Mighty Bright Baby Bright Clip On Night Light - Don't try to change a diaper in the dark, guys! But I also don't recommend turning on the full lights (a. because you don't want to disturb baby further and b. your husband/wife might be pretty ticked). We realized we needed these handy little portable lights on approximately Night 1 of being home with our newborn.

5. Fisher Price Snugapuppy Swing - Bless this thing.

6. SwaddleMe Wraps - It's cute to learn how to swaddle a baby with a blanket when you're in the hospital, but these wraps are the perfect newborn-sized burrito-makers, complete with velcro straps for fast and secure swaddling.

7. Carseat cover - Great for sunny stroller walks and car rides, and especially great when you finally venture out to restaurants. Just be sure to add a fan if the weather is very warm, as covers can raise the temperature up to 20 degrees!

8. WubbaNub - Adorable and older babies can use the stuffed animal to get the pacifier back in their own mouth. A total win.

9. Boppy Lounger - This also tops my list as an absolute must-have item. I actually have adopted this item as my signature baby shower gift (I think I've purchased 4 or 5 since writing this list!) Boppies come in cute prints, but I recommend buying a cover so you can remove it and wash it. I got custom covers made on Etsy, and now when I get the Boppy Lounger as a shower gift for friends, I always add a personalized

cover from this shop that matches the mama-to-be's nursery theme.

10. Regular Boppy - This was my BFF during the breastfeeding days, and then became a great tool for helping my daughter learn to sit up (placed around her back on the floor) when she was around 5-6 months old.

11. Simethicone Liquid - Sometimes babies cry because something is wrong with them, and we just can't figure out what it could be. Usually during those times, it's gas. Contrary to popular belief, gas can be caused by both breastfeeding and formula feeding. This medication helps by breaking up painful gas bubbles in the stomach and making it easier to pass. Lifesaver.

12. Gerber cloth diapers (use as burp rags) - I am definitely not a cloth diaper kind of gal (laundry is not my strong suit), but these things are way more practical and durable for cleaning up spit up than your typical cutesy-design burp cloth typically given at baby showers.

13. Friddababy NoseFrida - If (and when) you buy this, it will most definitely top your list of "weirdest new thing I do as a parent"- it's basically like a gas siphon you stick in your baby's nose and suck as hard as you can until the tube fills up with their snot. I'm not kidding. And you need it. Babies are obligate nose-breathers, meaning: if those tiny lil' airways get plugged up, they aren't happy, which means you won't be, either.

14. oogie bear - Have you ever tried to pick a tiny human's nose for them? Well, you will soon, and you need this perfectly compact booger-grabbing-stick to help you do it.

15. Tear-Free Bath Rinser - This is something you will use during baths for your newborn all the way through toddlerhood.

16. Gerber Sleep n' Play Zipper Onesies - Don't play with button-ups. Nobody has time for buttons during a 3AM diaper change.

17. UPPAbaby Cruz Stroller- It may be on the pricier side of stroller selections, but it is excellent quality, lightweight, easy to fold/unfold, and I love the matching carseat (see below) which easily snaps in and out of the stroller. The Cruz is a bit smaller than the more expensive UPPAbaby Vista stroller, but if you are wanting to make a stroller investment for future kids, the Vista can convert to a 2-seater.

18. UPPAbaby Mesa Carseat - This carseat easily clicks into UPPAbaby stroller, and has a very user-friendly design. The car installation for the base was straightforward and the instructions aren't hard to follow- always a plus.

19. Nest Cam - We love this system and still use it. The camera connects to your iPhone and you view it in the Nest app. You do have to have a strong Wi-Fi connection.

20. Dock-a-Tot - We found the transition to the crib from the bassinet was much easier using the Dock-a-

Tot, because it provides the same "snug" feeling that babies love.

If pumping:

1. Medela Pump in Style Advance (call your insurance before purchasing, they should cover it)

2. Medela Quick Clean Breast Pump and Accessory Wipes

3. Medela Easy Expression Hands Free Pumping Bra

4. Medela Quick Clean Micro-Steam Bags - not only are these a life-saver for cleaning the infinitely-dirty pump parts, you can also use these to sterilize pacifiers and bottle parts!

5. Kiinde Kozii Bottle and Breastmilk Warmer

6. Kiinde Twist Breastmilk Storage Starter Set - If you're planning to build a freezer stash or even store breast milk in the fridge, you need this. This starter set comes with twist-on attachments for basically every brand of pump out there, and then you simply twist on the storage bags and you pump directly into the bag. Close it up, organize it in your fridge with the included fridge rack, and you can even take it one step further and twist the bag into the included bottle attachment and feed it directly to baby.

If bottle or formula feeding:

1. Dr. Brown's Natural Flow Bottles - These have an internal venting system that helps to prevent gas.

2. <u>Baby Brezza Formula Pro</u> - If you are formula feeding, another absolute must-have item is this little machine sent from heaven. Think of a Keurig coffee-maker, for babies. You don't even need a bottle warmer because the bottle is made in less than 30-seconds at a perfect 98.6 degrees.

3. <u>Boon Lawn Drying Rack</u> - You're gonna be cleaning bottles like 57 times a day, and they need a place to dry. This is the place.

References

Aycock, D. M., Grissette, B. G., & Spratling, R. (2018). Barriers to help-seeking behavior among women with postpartum depression. *Journal of Obstetric, Gynecologic & Neonatal Nursing, 47*(6), 812-819.

Bingham, D. & Jones, R. (2012). Maternal death from obstetric hemorrhage. *Journal of Obstetric, Gynecologic & Neonatal Nursing, 41*(4), 531-539.

Mayo Clinic. (2018). Umbilical cord care: do's and don'ts for parents. Retrieved from https://www.mayoclinic.org/healthy-lifestyle/infant-and-toddler-health/in-depth/umbilical-cord/art-20048250

Made in the USA
Middletown, DE
16 September 2022

10526785R00049